PIT TALK

OF THE
EAST MIDLANDS

by
Natalie Braber
Claire Ashmore
Suzy Harrison

Natalie Ash

BRADWELL
BOOKS

Published by Bradwell Books
9 Orgreave Close Sheffield S13 9NP
Email: books@bradwellbooks.co.uk

British Library Cataloguing in Publication Data:
a catalogue record for this book is available from the British Library.

1st Edition

ISBN: 9781910551806

Design and typesetting by: Andrew Caffrey

Print: Gomer Press, Llandysul, Ceredigion SA44 4JL

Image Credits: iStock, The National Coal Mining Museum for England. Images credited separately.

Acknowledgements

We would like to thank Bradwell Books for agreeing to publish this book following our 'Pit Talk' project, and the British Academy for funding the project; without their support we would have been unable to carry out research and interviews. Thanks also to a range of other organisations and people. Nottingham Trent University funded the initial pilot project, and Chris Dann and Alice Cope carried out the very first interviews as part of this pilot.

The National Coal Mining Museum for England allowed us to use some of their excellent photos to illustrate our book; in particular Stephanie Thompson spent time showing us how to access the archives and helped with sorting the images. Also, Ross Williams allowed us to use one of his photos. Many individuals have helped us find information and checked facts when needed: David Amos, Ben Braber, Colin Hyde, the South Derbyshire Mining Preservation Group, Bilsthorpe Heritage Group, Pleasley Heritage Group, Julie Holling at Limestone House, Creswell, and miners at Thoresby Colliery, then still working, who spoke to us. Roger Cornish allowed us to use one of his poems in our book. Last, but certainly not least, we are grateful to all of the miners (and their families) who we interviewed – without them we would not have been able to produce this book. They have provided us with many hours of conversation, information and a lot of fun!

They are: David Amos, Bob Bancroft, Andrew Bown, Bob Bradley, Gary Brown, Ron Chaplin, Mick Chewings, Nev Clarke, David Coleman, David Cope, Kevin Cope, Roger Cornish, Clive Cottrall, Alan Dickson, Terry Foye, Steven Fullwood, Reuben Gregory, Brian Gunner, Dennis Jason Hall, Bryan Hallam, John Hardwick, Jim Harrison, Donald Hooley, Phillip Howe, David Jukes, Bill Kimberley, Anthony Kirby, John Knighton, Les Lovegrove, Betty Mapply, Lewis Marriott, Michelle Marshall, George Norley, Bill Parsons, Bob Patton, James Perry, Eric Purdy, Peter Rose, Ian Smith, Kenny Smith, Perry Taylor, Arthur Wheeldon, Roger Ward, Maurice West, Drew Wilkie, Brian Wingfield and Fred Whiting.

Introduction

We use the term 'Pit Talk' to refer to the language used by miners in their daily work. It is a language which is distinctive but is now at risk of being lost with the closures of the collieries throughout the country. This book aims to collect some of this language, used by miners of the East Midlands, to preserve it and to allow us to examine 'Pit Talk' in more detail.

When Natalie Braber moved to the East Midlands eleven years ago, working as a linguist who specialised in accents and dialects, she couldn't help but notice that almost no academic research had been conducted on the varieties of the language spoken in this region. In the course of correcting this oversight she spoke to local miners and discovered that many of the terms and words they used comprised a completely unique – and much overlooked – language variety. She also found quickly that the East Midlands had not one, but many variations of this 'Pit Talk'.

These discoveries warranted further investigation. In the summer of 2013, Nottingham Trent University awarded Natalie funds to engage two undergraduate students (Alice Cope and Chris Dann). They started interviewing local miners. We noticed straight away that much work needed to be done, but fortunately we also received a lot of media interest, and the publicity around our project attracted the attention of individuals and local mining groups who wanted to participate. So, together we were able to create a preliminary set of 'Pit Talk' items, such as words and expressions used by miners.

In 2015 the British Academy awarded further funding which allowed Suzy Harrison (a PhD student at Nottingham Trent University specialising in intangible heritage) and Claire Ashmore (a PhD student at Sheffield Hallam specialising in the language of Chesterfield, Derbyshire) to come on board for a full year.

During this year we were able to establish more links and contacts with former miners and mining heritage groups, and create a web page, open a Twitter account and conduct interviews across Nottinghamshire, Derbyshire and Leicestershire. The miners we interviewed had so much to tell us. We were able to gather a large amount of facts: not just words and expressions, but also information about the daily work of a miner, and life outside the mine.

Many of the miners and groups we encountered were as determined as we were to preserve 'Pit Talk' for future generations. For many years, the regional economy in the East Midlands was based on coal mining, an important part of local working life. With all the pits closed, this language and its heritage were in danger of being lost. Today, many local people are working to preserve the heritage and we want to add to their efforts. We realise of course that our work is unfinished, and we are setting up future collaboration to ensure preservation and assist in the education of the younger generation.

In this book, we have collected information from miners from different areas of the East Midlands. As you can see, people from across the region sometimes have different opinions – and they don't always agree with each other! We have also gathered additional information from books about mining, mining heritage and 'Pit Talk' in other parts of the country. Finally, we have accessed electronic resources. All the sources are listed at the back of the book.

In this small volume there is of course not enough space to cover every aspect of 'Pit Talk'. We had to limit ourselves to the creation of a mini dictionary and what we believe were the crucial elements of mining life. Some of you may feel that essential subjects have been missed and you may not always agree with the descriptions we have given, but we hope you're not disappointed with this book. It's a start and, as always, diversity is the spice of life – and, as you will discover, of pit talk. **ENJOY YOUR READ!**

From left to right, Suzy Harrison, Natalie Braber & Claire Ashmore, taken during the 'Pit Talk' event held in May 2016.

Taken by Leon Jackson

Pit Talk Dictionary

A

Abbutment – Where the roof of the mine comes down

A steady number – A steady job, not strenuous, which could also be referred to as 'bobbie's job'

Adit – Old term for an entrance to a drift mine

Addle – To earn

Advance – Method of working coal on long wall advance face; opposite of 'retreat mining'

Advance heading – Method of working a coal face with two ripping lips in advance of the face line

AFC – Armoured flexible/face conveyor, a conveyor belt made of steel; see also 'panzer' and 'stage loader'

After damp – A mixture of carbon dioxide and carbon monoxide which occurred after a methane explosion; see also 'firedamp'

After shift – The afternoon shift that ran from early afternoon to early evening, also referred to as 'afters'

Air crossing – An airtight channel to allow the air from the return airway to pass either under or over the intake airway. Must be airtight to avoid this air mixing with the fresh air in the mine ventilation

Air doors – Ventilation doors, used to divert air through the mine, also referred to as 'air lock doors'

Airway – Term used at Ollerton for 'loader gate'

Allowance coal – Coal supplied to miner for free, also referred to as 'concessionary coal'

Delivering coal. © Ross Williams.

Amain – Used for coal tubs which had broken free, referred to as 'mainer' in Leicestershire

Anderson (Strathclyde) – Coal-cutting machine, made in Scotland

Anderton Shearer – This shearer has a horizontally pivoted drum with picks along the barrel. As the machine moves away along the face the drum rotates at high speed, shearing down the coal which is gathered up and placed on the AFC.

Arch – Curved top girders that are bolted together to make an arch shape to support the roof

Assistant haulage corporal – Assistant transport manager

Aurora – Boring machine term, used at Pleasley

Aye up mi ode, y'alreet? – *Hello my friend, how are you?*

B

Back heading – A roadway being driven out

Back rip – Enlargement of a gate affected by severe geological interaction

Back rippers – Men who dug the tunnels (in some Leicestershire mines); but could also mean the men who removed the old supports and set new ones in a crushed roadway or gate affected by geological interaction

Back shift – Afternoon shift, but could sometimes refer to the late or twilight shift

Backfill – Waste material used to fill the void created by mining

Bad 'ole – Roof depression

Baiting – Removing dirt from the floor to give extra height to a roadway; see also 'dinting'

Balk – If you balk something, it stops something or holds something back

Banjo – A round shovel

Bank – This can be used to refer to the coal face (this is mentioned by some Nottinghamshire and Leicestershire miners) but it is also used to refer to the area around the top of the shaft at the top of the pit

Banksman – Man who worked on the surface (although some miners mention he could also work at the bottom of the shaft), operating the cage, taking the motties of men, and responsible for safety at the pit top. See also 'onsetter'

Bantle – The number of men riding on the cage at one time

Barkle – When dirt sticks to someone or something; for example, *'He always comes home barkled up from the pit!'*

Bat – Rock mixed in with coal, therefore 'bat picking' was to sort stone from coal manually

Batham clip – Attachment at the rear of the last mine car to secure to the haulage rope

Battleships – Big lumps of limestone found after a roof fall on the coal face, mainly used in Nottinghamshire mines

Beans – Small pieces of coal; see also 'peas'

Beat elbow – Painful swelling due to ingress of dust

Beat knee – Injuries men sustained to knees due to working on them for prolonged periods

Bells – Used mainly in North Derbyshire mines instead of 'caps' to describe what you would put on top of props

Belt – The conveyor transporting coal from the face to the shaft, latterly made from PVC following the Creswell disaster in 1950 when they were made of rubber

Best brights – Top-grade coal

Bevin – Term used for a shift spent at home through mechanical breakdown or bad weather

Bevin boys – Men who were conscripted into the mines rather than the forces during the Second World War from 1943 onwards

Big butty system – Old system where one man was in

charge of producing all coal by employing men and boys on behalf of the owner and could control labour and pay wages

Big heavers – Large mine cars capable of carrying one tonne of coal

Big hitter – An exceptionally hard worker; could also be called a 'pacemaker'. This term was also used for big production mines which produced over a million tonnes of coal a year. The opposite of such mines were called 'bread and lard' or 'bread and herring' mines, referring to the snap of poorer men.

Biscuits –Small wood or metal inserts placed between a prop and roof bar; see also 'caps', 'lids' and 'pads'

Bitting – Term used to describe a falling of dust, which could warn of a roof fault

Black damp – Air which has been starved of oxygen; can also be used for gas containing excess nitrogen and carbon dioxide, often found in low-lying or damp workings; see also 'choke damp'

Blasthole – A drill hole in a mine that is filled with explosives

Blend – Fine coal; see also 'slack' (Coal dust or very small pieces of coal; see also 'blend')

Blocks – Metal chocks to stop tubs rolling, called 'pinners' if made of wood; see also 'chock blocks', 'lockers' and 'drags'

Blue miners' tattoos – Scars miners would have from

coal dust being trapped in cuts

Boat – A large high-sided tub, used for taking coal out of the pit, a term mainly used in Leicestershire

Bobcat – Small digger used for carrying equipment

Bodger – A flat-ended spanner with a spiky handle

Bogie – Open-sided truck for carrying supplies, sometimes called a 'danny'

Box – South Derbyshire term for 'tub'

Brights – Good quality coal

Bull nose shovel – Shovel which goes into a point, making it easier to get under the coal according to Nottinghamshire miners, whereas Derbyshire miners state it is a shovel with a round end

Bull week – Hard-working and well-paid week before a holiday when miners would try to get extra overtime to boost their holiday wages

Bunkey – A small fault in a coal seam

Burglars and bobbies shift – Silverhill term for night shift

Butterfly – Platform on top of cage to allow shaftsmen to examine shaft sides

C

Cabbage head – Sits on top of a hydraulic pit prop (which has a round head) to help support the roof. Held together with 'cleats'.

Cage – Lift going up and down the mine shaft; it has other names, such as 'chair' and 'skip', but it is commented by some that 'cage' is the universal term used by most miners

Cank – A word with several meanings; can mean hard stone, difficult, mud or siltstone

Cap lamp – Battery-operated light worn on a miner's safety helmet with the battery carried on a belt, connected by a cable

Caps – Small wood or metal inserts placed between props and roof bar; see also 'biscuits', 'lids' and 'pads'

Car – Large tub or mine car; in Markham Colliery this was the term used for a 'manrider'

Catch knocker – Man employed to release the catch that holds the tubs back

Chair – Lift; see 'cage'

Chargeman – Experienced underground worker in charge of other men

Checks – Metal identification tags which miners would hand in when they went down the mine so it was known how many men were down the pit; see also 'motties', 'tallies', 'tags' and 'tokens'. Often these terms were still used even if modern mines used swipe cards.

Checkweighman – Man who checked and weighed the coal; normally there would be one representing the company and one representing the union to ensure fairness

Cheese block – Big wedge of wood acting as a safety device to stop tubs moving; could also be called 'cheeses'

Chock – A hydraulic chock (replacing wooden chocks) consists of a number of props (legs) which resist pressure from the roof. There were also three- or five-legged chocks and the five-legged chock included a middle leg. Later there were also full shield supports.

Chock blocks – A wedge-shaped piece of wood used by miners to stop tubs from running away (see also 'blocks', 'cleats', 'drags', 'lockers'), also used to refer to pieces of wood to support chocks by timbering up roofs, also be called 'chock nogs'. The term 'nuddies' was used specifically in Nr.3 Whitwick colliery.

Choke damp – See 'black damp'

Chopper – An axe, used in Leicestershire

Choppy – Hay for horses

Chummins – Empty tubs

Cleats – Wedges to stop tubs from moving; see also 'blocks', 'chock blocks', 'drags' and 'lockers', but in Nottinghamshire this term could also be used to refer to tightened props. These were props which were narrow at the bottom end and wide at the top

Clipper-on/off – Man who clipped tubs on and off the ropes

Clippo – Clipstone Colliery

Club – To be off work and claiming sickness benefit – said to be 'on the club'

Coal bagging – Delivering coal to the miners' houses

Coal cutters – Shearers for cutting coal

Coaling – Shovelling coal or face machine in production

Cobbles – Small bits of coal

Cock wood – Wood taken home to light the fire which would please the wife

Cockameg – A prop; the same as a 'sprag', used in Leicestershire

Cocker – Greeting term used to each other; see also *'duck'*, *'mi owd'*, *'mucka'*, *'sirree'* and *'youth'*

Coddy – Boss or miner in charge of stripping of a face, used in Leicestershire

Coffin – Huge piece of coal which blocked the conveyor

Corporal – For many jobs, the term 'corporal' would be used instead of manager (assistant haulage corporal; senior haulage corporal), perhaps to avoid the different pay scheme which would need to be implemented if these jobs were managerial. In Leicestershire it could also be used to describe the man who would lay the rails and the sleepers, and in Derbyshire it could also be used to describe the rail on the floor which tubs would run on

Cotter pin – Used in Nottinghamshire for the item used to couple tubs together

Cow – A long iron rod fastened to the last tub, acting as a safety measure in case of the rope breaking: the rod would stick in the ground and hold the tubs to stop them from moving

Creep – The lifting or rising of the floor in a seam where the coal has been removed, also known as 'floor lift' or 'floor blow'

Cross marra – The person who did your job but on a different shift, used in Leicestershire

D

Daffodil – Trainee miners or apprentices were referred to as daffodils as they wore yellow helmets

Danny – A flat trolley for transporting items below ground, also called a 'jotty'

Dataller – Man employed on day rate; at Markham this was also called 'Dad's Army' or 'Sore Heel Gang'

Datalling – Day-wage work; see also 'odd-working' and 'tagg'

Day-wage system – The payment system that superseded the butty system

Days regular – Working the day shift (there were two day shifts) on a regular basis, not working rotating shifts

Dead legs – A miner who was not 100 per cent fit

Deadman's handle – Safety device on haulage engine

Deputy – Men who had authority in the mine to tell others what to do and to enforce punishment if miners were not working; their job was to check for dangers, such as damp. Also the mine official in charge of safety

Desford chock – Hydraulic chock, so called as it was originally designed in Desford Colliery, Leicestershire, also known as a 'mushroom chock'

Dinting – Levelling out the floors if it lifts, called 'denting' in Leicestershire; see also 'baiting'

Dobber – Overtime, used in Derbyshire; see also 'knobs' and 'doddy'

Doddy – Overtime – used in Leicestershire. Could be used for an hour's overtime, or working late, or the amount of time to be worked to be able to claim a quarter of a shift overtime. See also 'dobber' and 'knobs'

Dog collar – Leather strap worn around the neck to carry a flame lamp when crawling

Dog nails – Large-headed, thick, steel nails for fastening rails to wooden sleepers

Dog on/off – Attach coal tubs to each other and to ropes

Dolly props – Hydraulic Props that are pumped up with a lever

Dosco – Coal-cutting machine which was capable of cutting hard strata

Dot 'eaps or dot 'ills – Slag heaps; see also 'spoil banks/ heaps' and 'pit tips'

Dotter – South Derbyshire term for 'tub'

Dotty britches – Dirty trousers

Double decker – Lift or cage with two levels

Image of a Dosco. Photograph courtesy of the National Coal Mining Museum for England. The Harold White Collection.

Drags – See also 'blocks', 'chock blocks', 'cleats', and 'lockers'. This term was also used in Derbyshire to refer to a steel safety device which would detach from a tub if de-railed

Drop warwick – Big steel girder on a weight with a trip mechanism to stop runaway tubs or trams

Duck – Term used to greet someone; see also *'cocker', 'mi owd', 'mucka', 'sirree'* and *'youth'*

Dudley – A miner's water container, could be steel or more recently plastic. Origin of term unknown, some said the name came from the company who made it, others where it was made. Many miners mentioned not having heard of this term before

Dumplings – Wooden blocks placed in the middle of the track to act as safety devices

E

Early doors – First shift of the day, also called 'early daze'

Early rider – Anyone who rides the shaft before the set finishing time, also referred to as being 'on a flyer'. 'Early rider' could also be used for men allowed to leave the pit early as they were very wet, or union men needing to attend meetings or union work.

Elephants' feet – Type of stilt set into the ground to raise the prop and give support

Elephant's tab – Big shovel for loading coal

Exemption – Term used at Ollerton to signify strict limit on men working at weekend - safety measure as it only had one escape route as it was not connected to any other pit underground

F

Face – Term given to the workings on an exposed face of coal where coal is being worked and extracted; also coal face or bank

Faced and arsed – Patching up trousers with other material

Feeder gate – Where equipment and men entered the mine - see 'main gate'. Uniquely used in Annesley to refer to return gate.

Firedamp – Explosive gas mixture whose chief constituent is methane (produced from decaying vegetable matter); see also 'after damp'

First draw – Refers to the first cage to take men back to the surface; there would often be a rush to be on this as, depending on the size of the cage, it could take quite a long time to get all the men back to the pit top; see also 'last draw'

Fitters – Mechanics or maintenance men

Flat – A nine foot piece of timber; a tree trunk cut in half. A term used in Leicestershire

Flat capper – Someone who had to work on the pit top for the day

Floor blow/lift – Where the floor moved upwards, also called 'creep'

Flyer – Short shift that started at 7am but finished at midday, used in Nottinghamshire

Fob – To hide something, used in Leicestershire

Foul tubs – Tubs containing coal unfit for sale

Fourteen-pounder – Size of hammer

Frit – Frightened

G

Gang job – Moving materials underground from one place to another

Ganger – Pony driver in older mines, but used to refer to a haulage worker in modern mines

Ganzi – Coat worn in the mines

Gate – An underground roadway leading to a face; these tunnels were referred to as 'gates'

Gate-side pack – A wall of stone or waste from gate-ripping debris built at the side of a roadway for support

Gean – An easy, good or profitable job: *'it's gean work'*, *'a gean shift'*

Get stuck in and get rid – Work hard

Get your fetlocks out – Get out of the way

Get your head down and your arse up – Refers to position taken when working hard

Goaf – Waste area; see also 'gob' and 'waste', also part of the mine from which the coal has been extracted and the roof allowed to fall in behind the coal face

Gob – Waste area created by removal of coal; see also 'goaf' and 'waste'. 'Gob it' could also be used to refer to throwing something

Gowl – Roof and sides were said to 'gowl' when they began to break down and cause trouble

Grabbers – Men who regularly work overtime

Grabbit – Snap time

Greenun – Throwing a sickie – *'havin' a greenun'*, used in Leicestershire

Groshel hammer – Hammer for knocking pins out

Gubbins – *'There was the gubbins at the backs of the supports which as your supports went forward the roof came down behind that*

it just fell down and collapsed at the back'; see also 'gob' and 'goaf'

H

Hammer – Sledgehammer rather than a traditional hammer

Hand-filling – Filling coal into tubs before full mechanisation

Hard getting – A face that is difficult to work and extract coal from

Haulage – Transporting materials inbye (from the chair to the coal face) or to developments

Headgear – Headstocks: steel construction over a mine shaft on which the pulley wheels are mounted. The pully wheels guide the cables from the winding gear, the cables are used to raise or lower the cages in the shaft

Heavy gang – Group of specialist heavy haulage workers

Hog back – Sharp rise in floor of coal seam

Hold down! – General warning to a miner to watch his head

Hold over! – General warning to a miner to watch to his side

Hold up! – Warning to men walking behind when there is a danger of tripping

Holer – Man who undercut the face, inserting small struts of wood to prevent coal from breaking away too quickly

Headstocks at Pleasley. © Suzy Harrison

Hollow pack – A pillar was supposed to be left standing to support the roof, but sometimes a quicker 'hollow pack' was built, from stone or 'rammel', to save time

Hopper – Container which held coal before it was weighed to deliver to people's houses

Hoppit – Small cage capable of carrying one or two men

Horned danny – A danny (trolley) with a pole on each corner, which could be made into a flat bed and could be used for hauling dirt, and could also be referred to as 'hutches' or 'tub'

Horseback – Bump in seam floor

Horse head clip – Used to clip things to railings

Hostler – Man in charge of the horses and ponies; or 'ostler

House coal – Bigger lumps of coal for domestic use

How's yer gert? – *How's your wife?*

Hunkers – Squatting down whilst working in low areas

I

Idle back – Safety feature which purposefully de-rails tubs in the event of a broken rope

Ilson – Ilkeston

In your black – Unwashed after a shift if a mine didn't have baths or showers

Men showering in New Lount, Leicestershire.
© Fox Photos, permission given by Getty Images.

Inbye – Towards the coal face, as opposed to 'outbye' (coming away)

Inrush – Water coming into the workings

Intake – Airway along which fresh air is taken into the mine, as opposed to the 'return' airway which carries foul air away

Irishman's rise – Derogatory term for being given a better job but without more pay

Iron-men – Coal-cutting machines

J

Jack catcher – A clip at the bottom of a tub, used to hold it in place, it would be released to let them move along the gates

Jacks – Used in Welbeck for 'cannel coal' where there was only one band of coal within a seam; in South Derbyshire it was often used to refer to a thin band of dirt that was often found beneath a coal seam

Jafnagged – Knackered, particularly used in some Leicestershire mines

Jazz rails –A sharp bend in a line of rails, which would throw tubs off the rail if going too fast

Jib – Cutting edge of the cutter

Jibber – Man who worked with the props

Jig – An incline where the counterweight of full and empty tubs is used to move coal, particularly in South Derbyshire. In other areas it could be used to refer to a steep incline.

Jigger pick – Pneumatic pick using compressed air, often just known as a 'jigger'

Jimmy crow – A tool used for bending rails underground

Jitty – A short passage connecting two roadways; see also 'snicket'

Jottie – A coal tub that was stripped to its chassis and then used for transporting material in the mine

Jumper – Sharp ended round bar or ringer for breaking down coal, in Nottinghamshire the term was also used for a sharpened metal bar used to make holes in the face to insert gunpowder

Jups – Term used at Thoresby for pieces of wood

K

Kank – Very hard (usually of material)

Keep a few men in their pockets – A deputy would have in his pockets the discs of men he could call upon to perform certain tasks

Keps – Steel blocks under the chair for the chair to rest on; could also be used to refer to the cage supports at the shaft top

Kibble – Could refer to anything from a very large bucket to a small cage which could be used to transport waste, material or men when used for cage and shaft repair, could also be called a 'hoppit'

Kinged – If a cage overshot it was said to have 'kinged'; this term comes from 'King's Patent', which was the safety device at the top of the cage to stop it hitting the headstocks and breaking the rope. Named after John King from Pinxton in Derbyshire, inventor of one type of detaching hook. See also 'overwind'.

Knobs – Overtime, also referred to as 'dobber' and 'doddy'

L

Lads – Name used to refer to the other miners; in some Nottinghamshire mines it was mainly used to refer to younger men and in some Leicestershire mines it was used to refer to apprentices

Lagging – Planks or small timbers placed between steel ribs along the roof to stop rocks from falling, rather than support the main weight of the overlying roof

Lagoon – Expanse of water surrounded by slurry

Lampman – Man employed to clean and maintain the lamps in the lamp cabin

Landsale – In Nottinghamshire this referred to the weighing bridge which could measure weight of coal mined, but in other areas it could also refer to coal sold for transport by road (as opposed to sea, canal or rail)

Last draw – Last cage ride of a shift; see also 'first draw'

Last man button – A switch at the pit bottom where the

onsetter can signal himself out of the mine

Length – A stretch of coal; in Leicestershire this is called a 'stint'

Lids – Inserted between support prop and steel bar; see also 'biscuits', 'caps' and 'pads'

Limmer – A contraption attached to a pony saddle to allow tubs to be hauled

Line lads – Men who painted lines on the roof to ensure the roads were straight; some miners commented that these men liked to call themselves Assistant Surveyors!

Lip men – Men who took the roof out to make it high, used in Leicestershire where other areas would refer to 'lipping' as 'ripping'

Loader gate – Where coal was loaded into tubs or onto a conveyor; see both 'main gate' and 'return gate' as used to refer to both in different mines

Lockers – Round steel bar or piece of wood to stop tub wheels moving, see also 'blocks', 'chock blocks', 'cleats' and 'drags'

Loco – Underground locomotive; see also 'manrider' and 'paddy'

Loco shed – Storage for loco, could be underground or above ground

Long Tom – A swing rail which formed a set of points to cause a tub to swap tracks

Long wall face – A name given to the coal face

(as opposed to pit and stall face) when coal was ripped in one go, rather than in particular 'lengths' or 'stints'

Loosall – End of the shift and time to go home

Lump – Big piece of coal

M

Main gate – Roadway where air, men, materials travelled towards the face, has many other names ('number 1 gate'; 'supply gate'; 'feeder gate'; 'loader gate'; 'mother gate'), some of which mean different gates in different mines

Main road – Gate road usually from pit bottom leading to coal-cutting district

Mainer – Leicestershire term for a runaway mine car

Man hole –Hole cut into the wall of a roadway as a safety refuge for getting out of the way of moving tubs

Manrider – Could be used as a name for the lift in which men travelled down the shaft in some areas, but was also used to refer to underground trains which transported men to the face (also known as 'paddy trains' and 'locos') or for conveyor belts which had been passed as safe for men to ride on; see also 'loco' and 'paddy'

Management tickets – System whereby a certain rank in the forces allowed a man to enter mining at management level

Managers – Those in charge of work in the pit

Men in cage. © Reynolds and Branson of Leeds 1910.

(started with managers, undermanagers and deputy managers – these were in charge of overmen – then deputies and then the workforce); the National Coal Board used to refer to 'Staff and Line Management'

Miners riding a man-riding car at Ellington Colliery. Photograph courtesy of the National Coal Mining Museum for England. The Harold White Collection.

Manchester gate – Name given to a gate which opened and closed again after the loco went through it, acting as a safety device as if any mining cars got loose they would bump into the gates and avoid injuring miners

Manips – Small bonus paid for less pleasant work (for manipulating less popular jobs)

Mashing can – Container in which to brew/mash tea

Maundrel – Tool with a pick at one end and a hammer at the other; see also 'noper', 'noser' and 'tadge/r'

Meal ticket – If you worked two hours' overtime on a shift, usually for a particular reason such as to provide cover between shifts or following a breakdown, you would get a meal ticket to get something to eat at the canteen

Mekadoddy – Extra quarter shift, about two hours; see also 'doddy', especially used in Leicestershire

Mell – Hammer weighing up to 14 pounds

Minecars – Large tubs of coal, from two to four tonnes

Mi owd – My friend; see also *'duck'*, *'cocker'*, *'mucka'*, *'sirree'* and *'youth'*

Mining optant – Official name for 'Bevin boy'

Moggy/pit moggy – Mentioned as being a local name for miners in Nottinghamshire, and also meant mice (as opposed to cat, which it means in many other regions)

Monday hammer – Heaviest hammer, said by some to be 'as popular as Monday', so not used if it could be avoided! Others stated it was called a Monday hammer, as if you used it on a Monday, you would be too tired to work on a Tuesday!

Mortek – Hammer; it was commented that it was only used at Rufford, and could be influenced by Polish miners

Mosh – Used for coal which was likely to break down during transportation, said to 'mosh down'

Mother gate – Other term for 'main gate', where men and materials would enter the mine

Motties – Metal tags which would be handed in at

different stages in the mine and could be used to count men in and out of the mine; see also 'checks', 'tags', 'tallies' and 'tokens'

A selection of 'motties', taken at John Knighton's house.
© Suzy Harrison

Muck – Coal waste product
Mucka – Friend; see also *'cocker'*, *'duck'*, *'mi owd'*, *'sirree'* and *'youth'*
Muscle in – Make a concerted effort to complete a task
Mushroom chock – Hydraulic chock; see also 'Desford chock'

N

Needles – Support props
Never carry stones – Don't bear a grudge, used in Leicestershire
Niffing – Overtime, used in Derbyshire

Nog – Wooden chock used to build packs

Noggin – Similar to a cleat, used as a wedge to prop something up. Also used to refer to quarter of an hour overtime worked.

Nomper – Metal bar used to knock clips onto tubs so they could be connected to one another

Noper – Tool which at the top end had a hammer on one side with a thin metal spike on the other; sometimes referred to as 'maundrels', 'nosers' and 'tadges/tadgers'

Noser – see 'noper'

Number one shaft – Where men and materials go into the shaft; see 'main gate'

Number two shaft – Where coal exists the shaft; see 'return gate'

Nuts – Small pieces of coal, also referred to as 'washed nuts'

O

Odd-working – Day-wage work, also referred to as 'datalling' or 'tagg'

Off the rod – Quarrel between two workmates (because of tools being stored on the same rod), used in Leicestershire

On the bank – On the surface; could also refer to being on the coal face

On the tonnage – Payment system that depended on the amount of coal a miner extracted, i.e. piece or contract work

Onsetter – Man at base of cage who signalled to the banksman when the cage was ready to move; see also 'banksman'

Outbye – Away from the coal face, as opposed to 'inbye'

Outloader – Men responsible for emptying coal into lorries to be taken away

Out-take – Where the cold air sucked into the mine to ventilate it would travel back out of the mine, usually warm!

Overman – Senior official usually in charge of an underground district, below undermanager but above deputies

Overwind – Where a cage is wound too far at the pit top and held in the headgear by the safety device; see 'kinged'

P

P4 – Name for a particular type of explosive (also 'P5' and 'Annabel', which were used for hard stone)

Pacemaker – Miners' term for exceptionally hard worker; see also 'big hitter'

Pack – Roof support consisting of debris surrounded by dry stone walls, usually at either end of the coal face

Pack hole – Area of the face where roof supports are constructed

Paddy – Train to take men into the pit; see also 'manrider' and 'loco'

Paddy pan – Bucket or tub for lowering water for horses

Paddy riding – To be transported on a paddy train

Pads – Pieces of timber placed between props and roof support timbers; see also 'biscuits', 'caps' and 'lids'

Paid snap – Small payment for working through a meal break

Pan – Coal scuttle-shaped container into which fillers rake small pieces of coal

Pan shovel – A round-ended shovel used on rough floors; also used to describe very large shovels

Panzer – Metal conveyor belt on the face used to transport coal out of the mine, from the German name for an armoured chain; see also 'AFC' (armoured face conveyor) and 'stage loader'

Pay loader – Large vehicle with a bucket at the front for scooping up coal

Peas – Small pieces of coal; see also 'beans'

Peck – In Leicestershire this term was used for both a shovel and a pick

Peck it out – Shovel it out, particularly when related to dinting – used in Leicestershire

Peg board – Board for hanging motties on when they

were handed in either when the miners were going down the mine or returning from a shift

Pig's head – Name for a particular type of drill which resembled a pig's head

Pigtail –A hook for a mine bucket in Leicestershire and in Nottinghamshire and Derbyshire for clips for tubs

Pillar – Mass of coal left to support the roof after excavation, or a pocket of coal left to support particular buildings above ground

Pillar and stall – Method of mining coal by leaving coal to support the roof between places where coal has been mined

Pin number – Miner's number chalked onto a tub of coal

Pinch bars – Crow bars

Pinned – If a man was 'pinned' he was trapped by fallen material, for example *'I've been pinned on my legs'*

Pinner – Used at Markham and some Nottinghamshire mines to describe a wedge that goes on top of a prop; see also 'chocks'

Pit bank – The surface of the mine; also used to refer to the spoil heap at some Leicestershire mines

Pit bottom – The area at the bottom of the shaft, sometimes simply referred to as 'downstairs'

Pit legs – Having common sense in emergency situations, also referred to as 'pit sense'

Pit mucks – Dirty clothes

Pit ponies – The ponies which were used to work in the mines, never referred to as horses

Pit tips – Slag heaps; see also 'dot 'eaps/'ill' and 'spoil banks/heaps'

Pitcher – Miner loading tubs at a loading point, used in Leicestershire

Play-in – To begin opening out a coal face from the side of a heading, used in Leicestershire

Pod – Flat car for transporting materials

Poll, Polly – Silverhill miner's name for his wife

Pom poms – General name for compressed air tools; refers to the noise they make which sounds like wartime naval guns

Popeye – Spanner for undoing the switchgear which tubs travelled on

Poppets – Valves on the trepanners: pressure release valves

Post – Wooden prop

Post-top – A solid roof which requires less support

Powder – Explosive material that requires a detonator to explode

Powder money – Extra payment given to the men who carried the explosives

Powder monkey – Man carrying bag of explosives or assisting shot firer for extra pay

Power loader agreement – Pay agreement for men working on mechanised faces with guaranteed wages (came in during 1966): the standardised wages agreement for coal face workers

Pre-shift – An inspection of the workings, by a safety official, usually a deputy or overman, **before men went down for a shift**

Pricker – Thin metal bar inserted into the gunpowder hole and removed to enable insertion of a fuse

Prop – A support between roof and floor, could be wooden or metal, the metal ones usually incorporated a hydraulic mechanism

A miner putting up a hydraulic prop at a colliery in Nottingham.
Photograph courtesy of the National Coal Mining Museum for England. The Harold White Collection.

Prop drawer – Tool designed to withdraw roof supports from a safe distance

Pull lift – A tool used to lift heavy objects, hung onto a ring and then a ratchet mechanism would be operated to lift the object

Puller-off – The man who takes the tubs off at the pithead

Putter – Man pulling or pushing tubs by hand; could also be used for men shovelling by hand

R

Radge – A pick with one of the blades forged into an axe; used to chop broken props when drawing the timber out

Ragarms – Nickname for a lazy worker, only mentioned in Derbyshire

Ragging up – Finishing the job and dressing to return to pit top

Raker – Big lump of coal; in Leicestershire this term could also be used of coal about to fall down over a ledge

Ram – Mechanical aid [usually hydraulic] used in the release of powered supports; can also be used for the device which pushes forward the conveyor

Rammel – Rubbish

Ramming – Putting explosive chargers into holes

Ram's head – A heavy boring machine that looked like it had horns. Would be used to drill shot holes; also called 'ramming stick' and 'rammer'.

Rat tail spanner – Spanner with long tapered end

Ratch – A length of coal face, about nine yards long, marked by the deputy with a chalk line on the roof which a group of miners would work on during their shift

Ratcher – A collier, used mainly in South Derbyshire and Leicestershire

Ratchet – Lever something up (particularly if heavy)

Ratching – Hand-filling

Relay bar – Connects panzer conveyor to a ram, used mainly in Leicestershire

Re-lighter – Safety lamp carried by deputies only, could be re-lit if extinguished unlike other safety lamps which did not have striking mechanism

Rembler – Man who broke the coal into manageable chunks

Resa – Reservoir, for example, Moorgreen Resa; could also be referred to as 'res'. See also 'rezza'.

Reservation – The local name given to the new housing estate at Ollerton provided especially for miners moving into the area

Rest day – Individually chosen day off, requested and approved officially

Retreat mining – When working back from the face and recovering the coal pillars that had been left during earlier stages, see 'advance mining'

Return – Where the used air comes out: 'intek and return'

Return gate – Return shaft; has many other names

('number two shaft', 'supply gate', 'tail gate', 'loader gate'), some of which have opposite meanings in different mines but generally meant the shaft which material and men would leave the mine

Rezza – Pit pond (spelling unclear, could also be 'Ressa' or 'Reser'; these differences suggest differences in pronunciations used by different miners); see also 'resa'.

Ricket – Narrow channel cut along the floor to drain off water

Riddle the slack – Sieve small bits of coal

Rider shaft – The term used at Snibston for the return shaft or return gate

Riding limmers – Illegal practice of riding on pit ponies; this term came from the word 'limmers', which was the harness which went around the pony's neck

Riding tubs – Term used when miners used tubs rather than walking to travel back to the cage. Generally prohibited because of the danger, but still done.

Ring off and let chair go – Used by miners to mean to get the lift moving, signalled by three rings of the bell

Ringer – Crowbars, which got their name from the noise they made when they struck rocks. *"They were four-foot crowbars with a wedge end to lever things up."*

Ringer and chain – Large iron bar with chain attached used for withdrawing props, also known as 'dog and chains'

Ringer bell – A Y-shaped piece of metal with a hacksaw

blade tied to it, used on the haulage rope so it would connect bell wires together to ring a bell at the engine house

Ringing on/ringing off – Terms used for bells and buzzers sounded to signify it was safe to begin winding the cage or used on the haulage system

Ring-rose lamp – Used to detect gases

Ripper – Miner who works on the roadway behind the face, sometimes called 'lipper'

Roadman's hammer – Special hammer used for laying rails (rare and so closely guarded); some miners comment it was like a 'noper'

Roadway – Underground tunnel

Roddin' up – Each miner had a rod with a slot for every tool which you could put away at the end of a shift, so 'rod up' would be to go back up and go home, used in Leicestershire. See also 'off the rod'

Roofin' – Where the roof was low or dropping and you could hurt your back

Rope capping – Inspecting the wire ropes which hold the cages and take the strain of lifting them up and down the shaft (the cages are suspended by wire ropes, the wire ropes are used to lift the cages up and down the shaft)

Rubber belt – A flexible conveyor belt; see also 'belt'

Runner – Leicestershire term for when the roof came in, in other areas used to describe a runaway tub

Run-round – Job where you take empty tubs from the

cage and push them away: very busy, with no time for breaks! Used in Leicestershire.

S

Sack wall – A wall built out of sacks filled with coal

Safety jacks – Safety clips to hold the cage at the top of the shaft

Scissors – The crossing in the tub tracks

Scotches – Brakes used to stop tubs; they looked like a little cricket bat with two niches in it the width of the rail

Scour – To drive a headway through the waste

Scowl – A tunnel through a face

Screens – Place where coal was sorted and graded

Scrubbing – Thin layers of soft matter such as clay embedded in coal

Scud – Coal dust

Scufting – Another term for dinting

Scuttle – A failure to complete a task: *'it's a scuttle'*

Seam – A bed of coal

Second means of egress – Alternative emergency route out of the mine

Self-rescuer – Respirator that miners carried in case of gas or lack of oxygen which would help them breath and give them time to get out of the mine. It converted carbon monoxide into carbon dioxide and was introduced in the early 1970s

Set the men out for who you'd wear – Refers to a chargeman choosing this team of workers

Setting – Sorting coal, also called 'stacking'

Miners sorting the coal inside Calverton colliery.
Photograph courtesy of the National Coal Mining Museum for England. The Harold White Collection.

Seven-pounder – Size of hammer

Shaft – Vertical passageway into mine

Shaft – Hand pick

Shaft iron – Thick, bent iron rod that attached horses' shafts to tubs

Shaft side – Where you would hand your tally in to the banksman before going down the mine

Shaker shoot – Coal would come off the face, down the conveyor, onto the shaker shoot and be loaded into the tubs

Sham – Vest and trousers worn in very hot mines; some miners comment it is a vest only. Particularly used in Leicestershire

Shearer – Revolving drum cutter-loader on a coal face

Shifter – Spanner with long tapered end; could also be used to refer a hammer or adjustable spanner

Shonky pit – A shaft with only one lift with counterweight rather than a second lift; for example, Teversal, as the upshaft was not big enough for materials. This term had also been used historically to refer to smaller pits.

Shooky – Acetylene lamp in use before electric lamps in the mine, used in Leicestershire

Shop – Workshop on surface for blacksmiths, welders, joiners, fitters and electricians

Shot firer – Person qualified to detonate explosives

Shovers-on and off – Men who shoved full and empty coal tubs onto the chair

Shuffle – Moving along behind the coal-cutting machine putting in chocks

Sink buckets – Buckets to collect money for the family of a miner who had died, also called 'death collection'

Sirree – Used to refer to another miner, for example when saying goodbye: *'see thee sirree'*; see also *'cocker'*, *'duck'*, *'mucka'*, *'mi owd'* and *'youth'*. Can be seen spelled many different ways in other references, for example, 'serry', 'surrey', 'sorri' and 'sithee'

Skip – Large container for raising coal up a shaft

Slack – Coal dust or very small pieces of coal; see also 'blend'

Slip – Grain in coal

Slogger – Name for someone who worked hard

Sloom – Wet mudstone or fireclay, also known as 'lommy'

Slot – Taking out earth with a pick from a face to allow you to go under it to get at coal

Slurry – Wet coal residue from washing coal in the preparation plant

Slurry pond – Reservoir [of slurry] outside the pit

Snaker – Man who pushed the panzer (AFC) forward, following the shearer or trepanner

Snaking – When tunnel does not go in a straight line

Snap – Food/lunch. This was probably the one word named by all miners where everyone was in agreement!

Snap time – Food break

Snap bag – Bag to put snap in

Snap box/tin – Box to put your snap in; this could be metal or plastic and tended to have a particular shape. Often made by ACME, and these ones would always be metal.

Snap cabin – Area where men could eat their food on the surface

Snap ticket – Food to be sent down by the canteen for men working overtime

Snibby – Snibston pit

Snicket – Small passage linking one part of pit to another; see also 'jitty'

Sounding – Assessing the safety of a roof by hitting it with a pick handle

Spare board – When everyone has been given their job to do in the mine and if you are the last one left, you get what is left. Men who didn't have regular jobs were referred to as 'market men'.

Spinney – Small shaft dropped into a mine

Spires – Thin layer of coal in a clay mine

Spitchcl – Tool for removing coal cutting tools from the coal-cutting machine when they were worn away

Spoil bank or spoil heap – Waste material, dirt tip; see also 'dot 'ills/'eaps' and 'pit tips'

Spoon shovel –A long handled shovel with a small, oval, cupped head

Spotter – A lamp with extra bright spotlight to shine a long distance

Sprag – A prop put in at an angle; could also be called 'spragget' or 'stanger'. If you undercut coal you would need to 'sprag it up' so it didn't come down

Sprags – For the cage to sit on when at the top of the shaft

Sprog – Young apprentice, first year at pit

Sputnik – Compressed air borer; miners would say *'send the sputnik up'* as it was a long cylinder

Square nose – A square-ended shovel used in good conditions

Stable hole – Excavation usually at the gate end of a coal face to enable the cutting machine to be turned or moved over for cutting in the opposite direction to allow for depth of cut

Stack out – Dam off or close up the entrance to the waste by building a wall of stone or coal

Stacker – Butty employed on surface to empty tubs and grade coal

Stacking – Sorting coal, also called 'setting', used in Leicestershire

Stag – Short for 'nystagmus' – eye disease caused by working in low light conditions

Stage loader – A small armoured flexible conveyor belt for moving coal and materials, from AFC to conveyor

Stall – Working area of coal face

Standage time – Shift time for which payment could be claimed whilst there was a machine breakdown or other hold-up

Standing – As in *'why are we standing'*: *'why has production stopped?'*

Stang/Stanger – Long piece of wood used as a safety device to stop tubs rolling; also used to leaver tubs back on to the rails in the case of a derailment

Star clip – A device for fastening tubs to a steel haulage rope by hammering it closed/open; see also 'swan clip'

Steady number – A steady job, not strenuous, which could also be referred to as 'bobbie's job'

Stemming – Blocking off holes between tunnels using plaster-like material to stop undesired air venting

Stink damp – Hydrogen sulphide or sulphur dioxide;

smelled like rotten eggs

Stint – A set distance along a coal face allocated to a miner as his particular task in pre-mechanisation days

Stone shovel – A shovel with a wide blade

Stop lock – Safety device to stop a runaway tub; some would call this a 'dumpling'

Sump – Bottom of the shaft, below landing level

Supply gate – Term used to describe both 'main gate' and 'return gate'

Surface – Pit top

Swamp the loader gate – If coal is not cleared away and starts to build up

Swan clip – A safety clip; see also 'star clip'

Sweetdamp – Another name for carbon monoxide gas

Sweetener – Good-quality coal from another source mixed with poorer coal to improve the grade

Swillet – Undulation in roadway where water would gather; also called 'swilly'

Sylvester – Safety device for removing props

T

Tackle lads – Men involved in transporting materials

Tadge – A pick on one end, and a cutting blade on the other; could also be called a 'maundrel', 'noper', 'noser' or 'tadger'

Tadger – see 'tadge' above

Tagg – Day-wage work, also referred to as 'datalling' or 'odd-working'

Tags – Identification disks; see 'checks', 'motties', 'tallies' and 'tokens'

Tail gate – Opposite of the main gate where material and men would travel out of the mine; see 'return gate'

Tail rope – The haulage rope exposed at the back of the last tub

Tallies – Metal tags which would be given at different stages in the mine and could be used to count men in and out of the mine; see also 'checks', 'motties', 'tags' and 'tokens'

Teck a rack off! – Slow down!

Testing flame – A flame which could detect methane gas in the airstream

Thonking – Knocking a steel prop

Thunder box – Used as a toilet down the mine, found in pit bottom area only, not plumbed in but a box which would be emptied from time to time

Timber drawers – Men, mostly in their sixties, who would pull out supports and allow debris to drop into the gob

Timber leader – Deputy in charge of distributing timber to his workmen for setting supports

Timber up – Wooden planks attached to ensure chocks were secure

Tokens – Identification disks; see also 'checks', 'motties', 'tags' and 'tallies'

Tommyhawk – Combined pick and hammer, also referred to as 'tomahawk'

Tool rod – Eighteen-inch-long piece of material which tools could be put on

Top deck – The upper deck on a cage for men, materials or coal

Total caving – Where machinery is used instead of men

Trams – Underground wagons down the mine used to transport material

Trapper – Boy who controlled ventilation by opening and closing a door in pre-mechanised mines

Travelling time – Time allowed for travelling to and from your place of work at the coal face from the pit bottom

Trebles – Lumps of coal, also called 'cobbles', used at Calverton

Trepanner – A machine that travels along the face cutting out very large chunks of coal

Trolley – Low, flat truck used for manriding

Trowin – Plastic pipes which circulated air around the pit

Truck – Bigger than a tub

Tub – Coal tub, underground wagon

Tub shop – Area where equipment went in for repair

Tub thumper – Man who mended tubs if they were knocked out of shape or broken

Tweggies – Straps under the knees to stop dirt and dust entering the trousers, also known as 'yorkies'

Twilight – Late afternoon shift

U

Udged – Sounding hollow when the roof was tested by tapping with a hammer: 'knock udged'

Uncoupling block – Safety device that separated two tubs (so you could put your head between them and not get injured)

Undercut – A section of the base of a coal seam which has been cut away by hand to make it easier to bring the rest down by hand or with explosives

Undermanager – In charge of all underground operations

Up-cast shaft – Shaft where materials and men would usually travel up

Utility men – Popular members of the workforce who were very adaptable

V

Visitor speed – Speed at which a cage moves when occupied by visitors not used to the experience, to give them a fright! Could also be called a 'fast draw'.

W

Waiting-on time – Shift time for which payment could be claimed whilst waiting for a job to be prepared

Wall – The face

Warwick – A safety device for tubs, to stop them rolling down hills

Waste – Area left behind after coal has been removed; see also 'gob' and 'goaf'

Watcher – Experienced miner who would inspect the mine with the Deputy on a Sunday on behalf of the men

Water ingress – A waterlogged mine

Water money – Small extra payment for working in wet conditions

Wax walls – Thin lining of clay on sides of roadways for sealing pack walls to prevent spontaneous combustion

Wet notes – Records of periods spent in wet working conditions for which extra pay would be given

White finger – This is caused by prolonged use of boring or vibrating machines, the fingers lose colour and become numb

Whitedamp – Another name for carbon monoxide gas

Why are we standing/stood? – Said when the conveyor stopped working, or during a hold-up in production

Wind – Pull up and down the shaft

Winder – Someone who operated the cage in the shaft, also called a 'winding engine man'

Windless – A place in a mine where air is bad or in short supply

Windy pick – Hand-held compressed air jigger pick

Wood, The – Name for Nailstone Colliery

Wriggly tin – Corrugated iron sheets of metal, used in Nottinghamshire

Wristwatch and shopping bag pit – Term used for Calverton Colliery, where men wore watches and took their snap in bags rather than tins

Y

Yard stick – A walking stick carried by all mine officials, seen as a symbol of authority, used to test the roof of the mine

Yark – To jerk the winding rope

Yed in – To advance in

Yellow rest days – Relates to Statutory Sick Pay paid to employees for first seven days of illness; so called as the form is yellow. Also known as 'yellow perils'

Yorks or Yorkies – Knee strings worn by miners to keep trouser bottoms out of the mud; see also 'tweggies'

Youth – Common local term in Nottinghamshire for friend. Mentioned by some miners as being disliked by Scottish miners. Could be used as part of a greeting: *'what's up, youth?'* See also *'cocker'*, *'duck'*, *'mi owd'*, *'mucka'* and *'sirree'*

The Life of a Miner

As we stated in the introduction to this book, the deep coal mining industry has now ended in the East Midlands, and in the UK overall, but the importance of preserving our knowledge of this way of life and language is important. Angela Franks, when writing about Nottinghamshire miners, states that although monuments to mining are appearing, it is important to preserve other aspects of this culture as memories can be so short-lived that it may only take a generation for them to be lost. Through words, she says, we can save them for posterity.

For many years, miners' language has been an enigma to others. In 1724, Daniel Defoe commented when visiting a coal mine not only that *'the man was a most uncouth spectacle'*, but that when he described the tools that he used, *'not one of the names … we could understand but by the help of an interpreter'*. W. Forster comments when writing about mining in the South Midlands that miners developed their own language and that it is a mixture of local dialects and technical mining terms. He goes on to say that the language expresses a miner's whole culture and that their voices are a 'common consciousness'. We would like to give you the opportunity of experiencing this mining language by using the words of our miners – we have focused on some particular aspects of interest in a miner's life, including camaraderie, language used for particular tools and jobs and the dangers of the working conditions. We couldn't use all the stories – there were so many we could have included and we were sorry to have to miss so much out!

Language

Many of the miners we interviewed said that colliers from other areas spoke differently and that in certain instances this could lead to some confusion. Bryan Hallam states: *'When I first moved from Rawdon to Whitwick I found some of their terminology quite alien because I couldn't understand what they were saying.'*

There isn't very much that all the miners we spoke to agreed on, but one of the few words which is used without exception is 'snap' for food. This is also a word which is used widely outside of the mines, for example in miners' families, but it also seems to have spread beyond the mining community. One of the many examples we were given of this word was by Lewis Marriott, who comments that miners had *'Snap; we had a snap tin and dudleys as well.'* Interestingly, the dudley (which was a water container taken into the mine) was not universally agreed upon. Some miners said they had never heard of it, and even those miners who did use the term could not agree where it had come from. The miners often had different birthplaces and came from dissimilar areas; many men had travelled, not only within the East Midlands and around the UK but also further afield. Roger Ward comments on something he noticed when he was training. He says, *'When you first went to the training college, because they came from Leicestershire side and Derbyshire side, and we all made mates and we'd pick their lingo up and they'd pick our lingo up.'*

David Jukes adds, *'We did have a large influx of Geordies and Scots in at one time so a lot of the words that they used have kinda been adopted as well, you know, as these people came down onto the estates and started working down the mine. But I think they generally adopted our terms and language as opposed to the other way round.'* Fred Whiting confirms that at the mine he worked in, Cotgrave in Nottinghamshire, there were many 'Geordie miners', and Ian Smith, who worked in South Leicestershire, adds that there was also much influence from *'Scottish miners, who used to have the Scotch estate and the Rangers Club for miners from Scotland'*.

David Amos also notes the influences outsiders' language could have on miners. He comments that *'lots of the pits in South Notts, particularly in our side round here, had got strong cultural links with Derbyshire where there was older mining; lots of Derbyshire miners brought their terminology with them, and the accent, which was slightly different to mine – similar, but slightly different.'*

Kevin Cope mentions that the fact that the mines were such an integral part of the East Midlands economy makes this language significant. He says, *'Only Nottinghamshire language, I mean, is part and parcel of pit talk because it was such a big industry and in Nottinghamshire I should say it was the biggest industry … and I would say that the Nottinghamshire accent [ties in] with pit talk, it's all linked into one.'* The same of course could also be said for Derbyshire and Leicestershire, where the pits were the main employers in the region.

There are many examples where miners tell us about specific words which were used differently by the pitmen. Bob Bradley comments: *'Well, that gate used to be called "D-gate" at Teversal area. Delivery-gate, D for delivery. At other places it were called "mother gate", now why "mother gate" I don't know. And then at Ollerton it was always called "airway". The return gate, although they changed the air out they called it the airway so it was like "57's airway". I wondered what they were on about when I went there.'* Steven Fullwood tells us: *'At Dormill they called pit top "bank", which was strange to us. It was just pit top to us where at other places the bank could be the face. At Cotgrave the bank was the face. It can be confusing, strange. Then you talk to some older miners and they've got different words totally. I mean like an adjustable spanner, a shifter and things like that.'* And Clive Cottrall comments, *'We called it a cage, some people call it a chair.'*

Camaraderie

The camaraderie between miners is well known. D.H. Lawrence wrote in 1936 that the continual presence of danger in the mines made the contact between the men particularly close and that this was strongest down the pit. This 'brotherhood', as some of our miners refer to it, was one of the most common themes in our interviews. Many of the men comment that they did not necessarily enjoy all the jobs in the mine or like all the miners they worked with, but they all felt the strong bond between them. The dangerous working conditions that were part of everyday life necessitated such a fellowship between miners.

For many of our miners, working down the pit had been part of the family's history. James Perry comments that his dad was a miner, as were two of his brothers and four half-brothers. He mentions that he liked working in the pit and had lots of friends there. Phillip Howe's father was a miner, as was his brother. But even for those who didn't work with their family members, fellow miners were a crucial part of their lives. Bryan Hallam says that camaraderie didn't finish in the pit: you did everything with these men, in fact *'it was more family than anything, you were literally like brothers, you always got somebody watching your back. You know, to be quite honest, I've seen people go down the road, have an argument, go down the road and knock three bells out of one another and come back and that's it, passing a prop, job done. Miners never ever carry stones, because you never know what's going to happen tomorrow.'* Kenny Smith agrees with this: *'You could fall out with each other but if anybody was in trouble they were there.'*

Michelle Marshall, who worked in a pit canteen, says, *'Because everybody had somebody – it was uncles, it weren't just fathers and sons, it was uncles; everybody seemed to be related in some way – and because of the difficulty with going down the pit and obviously they knew that every time they went down it was a big risk to their health and to survive really. They had to trust each other, especially when they worked closely with each other.'* David Coleman adds that miners had to look after each other, *'And that's how it was down the pit. It wasn't just in the pit, the community itself on the pit top was so strong.'*

Some feel that the working conditions were an important factor in this closeness. Kevin Cope says, *'Life down the mine was rough, it was depressing. The only thing that actually kept you going down the pit was the camaraderie with your friends and your workmates down the pit. Apart from anything else, it was horrible.'* An important part of this camaraderie was 'the banter' and mickey-taking which many of the miners commented on. Anthony Kirby thinks that *'What people miss most with the pits closing is the banter. You miss the mickey-taking. It doesn't mean anything, 'cos you're looking out for each other.'*

One of the miners we interviewed had just finished his last shift at Thoresby a few days before. Steve Fullwood says, *'When we are underground we look after each other. If someone is struggling you help them and that's how it is. You wouldn't get by without looking after each other. The closeness of it.'* Many of the men we interviewed said that they still miss this way of life and the friends that were part of it. Perry Taylor says, *'I miss the friends'* and Kevin Cope thinks that *'No, there's nothing the same as what there is with a gang of pitmen working together.'*

Several miners comment that they would go back to mining if they could. Bob Bancroft states that *'If Bagworth pit had still been open I'd have still been there. I loved it. I had good mates … There was no, you know, like lay and struggle. None of that. Or if you've seen a tub off the rails, you used to go and help pick and put it back on. You'd never walk by. You'd never see anybody struggle.'* Gary Brown thinks his days in the mine were the *'Best years of my life, I loved it. Absolutely loved it with a passion. If I could go back now, I'd go back now. That's the passion, you know what I mean? My kids say, you're mad because it's made me deaf. I've got emphysema, I've got white finger, I've got my knees, I've got arthritis in this one now. But, I would still go back and do it.'*

For many miners, this close relationship with their colleagues is reminiscent of a different way of life. David

Coleman adds *'If you had nothing you'd give them half of it. That's how it used to be.'* And Bob Patton adds that *'Everybody spoke to each other, everyone said "You all right mate"; in fact you used to get a dry throat from saying hello as you used to walk in and walk out; that went when the old miners went, that camaraderie went.'*

It seems though that this camaraderie affected more than just the work carried out at the pit. Many of the men (and their families) took part in activities outside the mine that were still very much part of pit life. These included sports, music and social events, holidays organised and paid for by the pit and the 'welfare', the bar and the social hall where many events took place. Dennis Jason Hall remembers, *'I ran the football team for 22 years, no 28 years, and we won 122 trophies; we'd got three teams, like. It was the Coal Board; this pit in particular provided everything. Sawdust to mark the ground out, then we progressed to lime, the nets, the pegs – everything. The paint for goalposts. The pit provided everything for us.'*

Arthur Wheeldon also comments on the opportunities: *'Historically brass bands were popular, Bilsthorpe never had a brass band but there was one at Clipstone and Thoresby. Racing pigeons, football, cricket.'* And Ron Chaplin adds., *'All the collieries used to have good dance halls, particularly at Ollerton.'*

Derbyshire miners welfare holiday in Skegness. © National Coal Board.

Danger and working conditions

Many stories we heard relate to accidents and near misses. Brian Gunner tells a story of the time when he had a very near miss. *'Coming down the – what do you call them? – shaft in the cage, one night, come down to the bottom I put one leg off and somebody pulled me back as it shot right back up again. So I could have lost me leg. That was very close.'*

Donald Hooley recalls a time when he was supposed to be working but had the day off and his friend was working instead. The next day, he was waiting for this friend before work but the man didn't show up. He learned that his friend had been killed at pit bottom the day before. Donald comments, *'And I always think if I hadn't had the day off …'* Dennis Jason Hall explains that one of the biggest dangers in the pit was accidents with the tubs: *'Getting in between them, you know, cadging, getting rides on them and slipping.'* It seems that many accidents were avoided through 'pit sense', understanding subconsciously how the pit worked and knowing when something was about to go wrong. Some of the men mentioned that the pit ponies frequently had such a sixth sense. But miners also did, as Drew Wilkie comments: *'I believe there is such a thing as pit sense because the number of miners that will tell you, 'I just stepped back, something told me.'*

Many of the miners we interviewed reflected on the sometimes horrific working conditions down the mines. It could be intensely cold. Maurice West explains that Cadley was a drift mine and could freeze solid. In winter mornings it would be the job of one of the miners to break the icicles before the manrider could run. Peter Rose worked in a similarly cold mine. He says, *'There are cold places down the pit, really cold an all: at bottom of intake shaft it used to freeze over. You had two coats and a donkey jacket, two or three pair of trousers on. You could hardly move 'cos you had that many clothes on.'* The mines could also be extremely hot, or changeable depending on where you were working. Perry Taylor comments, *'Some places all you did was you wore your shorts and boots because it was that hot you'd just be wet through. You'd be wet through just opening your snap box up. But then sometimes on a Friday night, you'd go down perhaps in just your shorts and boots expecting to go onto the face where you'd normally work, which would be sort of 110, 120 degrees and perhaps that face had broke down or been pulled off and you'd be sent to one close to the pit bottom which would be a cold one and you'd have a cold wind blowing through and be frozen in your shorts.'*

Extreme temperatures were common, and some mines were also wet. Bryan Hallam explains that *'We started work at 7 o'clock and by half past seven the water was coming out the top of my waders. It was sodden; you could hardly move 'cos you were that wet.'* Bill Parsons also experienced this. *'We was drenched and they used to give us a concession – say about twenty minutes – because our clothes were that wet they wouldn't dry in lockers, you see, and when they were drying, when they dried in a locker you used to sweat muck and they would stand up like that, they would honestly they were that stiff, so they gave us another place to put them in and we used to take 'em in there. They were the worst conditions, the worst faces I've ever, ever worked on.'* Roger Cornish recalls working in wet conditions in the 1970s and suffering from wet bell-bottom flares! Wet mines could lead to more than just getting wet. Peter Rose described the situation of a mine where he worked: *'This pit had a few wet spots but not a lot.*

Some faces had all time wet, some now and again, but some had a lot of water, terrible. Gives you a tan you hadn't got because of the rust on the props and you get it all over your body and it doesn't wash off.'

There wasn't always much space to move around. Kevin Cope explains. *'It started soon as you got off the chair at pit bottom, 'cos the roadways as you were going down were quite high but as you got down the gateway towards the face, they got lower and lower and lower and sometimes you was actually crawling on your belly. You'd have to take your lamp off and your snap bag, you'd chuck them through a hole and then crawl after them 'cos it was that low. And you'd got down and it was hot, and humid, and dusty, it was just so depressing, but you was with all your friends and that's what made it bearable.'*

And obviously the mine was dirty. Andrew Bown says that before many mines started issuing orange overalls in the early 1980s, miners had to supply their own clothing and this would get filthy. As well as dirt, some mines also had unwanted animals in them. Drew Wilkie claims that *'Tilmanstone never had ponies at all so we never had vermin but South Leicester was full of mice. Tilmanstone had crickets. Millions and millions of crickets, which was strange; hoppers they used to call them. They would fly towards your light.'* Bill Kimberley discovered the unpleasant results of having vermin underground: *'Often if you'd forgot your snap tin and you took a couple of sandwiches quick and put them in your pocket or hung 'em up you'd go back at snap time – if you did have a snap time – and you'd see mice had been at them so you'd just throw that bit away and eat the rest.'* Many mines had pit ponies, which were liked by some men, as Les Lovegrove explains: *'In the canteen I bought two packets of Spangles; one were for pony. I just spoiled him; a lovely horse, Jim, white, a lovely white horse.'* Not everyone was as keen on these ponies, however. Dennis Jason Hall explains, *'They used to stand in a line like that and when you went by one to get to water trough they'd back out and they wouldn't move, the buggers; they knew you were scared of them. 'Cos we were only kids.'*

The work was physically tough. Roger Cornish describes how exhausted the men could get. He says, *'I used to shake, it was that hard. You know, your blood sugars were so low because you were working that hard and I used to think I'm not going to be able to do this. But you wouldn't give in because you didn't want your mates to think, you know. But eventually you develop a style of shovelling from the experienced miners that's quite easy. It's only shovelling you say, but you just do it for six hours. It was tough. But eventually you harden up to it.'*

The shift-working patterns could also be unsettling. Terry Foye says, *'It's strange being on three shifts because you go to bed, you wake up, and before you open your eyes you think, is it morning, is it day or is it night? And it took from Monday to Wednesday to get used to that rota, and following Monday you were on a different system.'* The life of a miner was hard and gruelling. John Knighton recalls, *'If I said it was a young man's game; I mean I've seen some old miners who's retired, and they used to say hard work never killed anybody, and I said no, but it twists them into some funny shapes.'*

Job Descriptions

These men, as well as coming in some funny shapes, did all sorts of different jobs. Miners themselves could be referred to as 'pit moggies' or 'colliers'. There were back rippers and belt drivers, banksmen, dinters, hauliers, fitters, lipmen, sinkers, onsetters, panzer drivers, face men and pit bottom lads. Some men worked above ground, some below and some a combination of the two. Miners learned from each other the jobs which had to be carried out. Everybody had to start somewhere and the novices were easily spotted in the mine. Perry Taylor comments: *'Daffodils were trainees. Trainee miners always wore yellow helmets so we used to call them the daffodils.'* This was a stage most men were keen to leave, Reuben Gregory said, *'We used to have a yellow hat, a red hat and a white hat. A yellow was like a baby apprentice, 'cos they used to have loads of accidents; as soon as you were qualified you used to get straight on to the white normal hat.'*

Some men do have happy memories of their first jobs, as

Eric Purdy explains. '*Started in 1947 at Bilsthorpe; first job was in the hard gang mashing tea for a gang of men that used to get materials into the pit. Making sure, especially in winter, that the stove was red hot and the tea was mashed on time and the cabin was swept out nicely and all that sort of thing. A good set of men, probably one of the best sets of men as I ever worked with, being a young lad at the pit; first job it were brilliant. They were very good to me. Especially at holiday time, every week they'd give me threepence a man and there was probably about eight in the group and they gave me threepence a man on the Friday to spend; that were a lot of money.*'

Many then progressed to working underground and there were a lot of different jobs to be carried out there and numerous things to be learned. Not all coal could be used, or used for the same purposes. As Alan Dickson tells us, '*They never bothered with the shale one because it was rubbish, rubbish coal. The top hard had finished when I started. The low main coal was very, very good. Most of the low main coal used to go to Ireland to the brick works, because it was high in something and low in ash. And the yard seam was house coal and the low main coal.*'

John Knighton explains what he used to do: '*When I first started there I worked in a pit bottom and I used to steady, with another man, steady the tubs as they came down the incline and went round a corner so that when they were loaded they didn't spill the coal all over the place or you had to clean the spillage up. And I thought to myself, I don't fancy doing this for a long time.*' Jim Harrison also remembers his first job: *'When you went underground you started in pit bottom. Then you went pit pony driving. Then you went onto the coal face … You were twenty or twenty-one when you went on face; well I was anyway – twenty. The manager used to say you can't go on yet 'cos your bones aren't set properly. You had to get some strength. You are talking about eighteen to twenty ton of coal a day with one of them big shovels.'*

The pony stables inside of Calverton colliery. Photograph courtesy of the National Coal Mining Museum for England. The Harold White Collection.

Many of the jobs required real skill. Roger Cornish admired these miners. He says, '*There were the old skills like the saddler: they'd sit on the saddle and they used old conveyor belts and they'd make pouches for explosives, and pouches for methanometers. Really skilled blokes, you know. Make the odd job for somebody at home, a bag or anything, you know. Then there's the sawmill … there's a roaring wood fire in there and in the winter everyone used to gather round that and they used to make their bacon sandwiches and all sorts. It was really, really homely sort of blokes, mother pit sort of thing.*'

The work that was carried out in mines changed over time with mechanisation and new inventions. Lewis Marriott describes one of these changes. '*Stinting is in the early days, before we'd got armoured face conveyors. A coal face would probably be two hundred yards long and each man would have a ten-yard stint, or eight yards depending on the thickness of the coal. The night shift would go along and undercut it with an undercut machine: that was a sort of five-foot bite all the way down the two hundred yards. The day shift would bore it, one or two shot firers on duty then and they'd stem all the holes, put the dynamite in, fire it, and the men would go along with a shovel and load it onto the belt. That was stinting. Then the afternoon shift would do a turnover. That's when they had to move the conveyor forward then do the same again.*'

Certainly not all men were equal in the mine and there were very specific hierarchies. John Hardwick explains: '*So an undermanager is responsible for everything in the pit, development work for putting in new faces, that sort of thing. Overmen, as the word says, were over most of the men. Deputies were responsible for a face or part of a pit. They might have a deputy who's in charge of the pumps over the men who were running the pumps. Shot firers were certainly a cut above the colliers, like.'*

Tools and Equipment

Not only did job titles and job descriptions have their own unique names, but the terminology used for the miners' tools and equipment was also both varied and distinctive. There are bodgers, lockers, nopers, pecks, dumplings, mells, shifters, cocks, panzers and tommyhawks. As Brian Wingfield says, *'Every tool had a different name.'* David Cope adds, *'I guess there were tools that I'd never heard a specific name for, so men used to make names up for them. Sometimes it was because of what the tool looked like, and sometimes they made no sense at all. For instance, there was the tool they used to use for taking coal-cutting pips out of the coal-cutting machine when they were worn away, and for some reason they called it a "spitchel", which never made any sense to me at all.'*

Some of this variation is shown and cross-referenced in the dictionary. It seems that different miners used different words for their tools. Sometimes the variance was to do with geography (miners in Derbyshire, Nottinghamshire and Leicestershire would use different terminology), but they could also be specific to individual mines. Even within one mine, there could be inconsistency. Mick Chewings states that *'In Cotgrave you had shaddel, you had elephant tab, you had banjo and you had another one and that was just four names for a shovel.'* One of the terms which has many alternative forms was the word used for the bits of wood (or metal) which would be put into the wheels of the tubs to stop them rolling away. They could be lockers or cleats, wedges or cheese blocks. Lewis Marriott gives one example. He says, *'When a tub used to run away you'd put lockers into it to stop it. You used to have wooden lockers and steel lockers. We used to have lashing chains as well but there wasn't so many. We were trained to use lashing chains. Clips was the most modern way of transporting tubs on endless ropes. A lashing chain was like an overhead rope about twelve foot long attached to the tub. They lashed it round the rope and it snatched it and dragged the tub. Lots of fingers damaged then.'*

The conveyor belt which carried coal out of the mine also had different names. Nev Clarke remembers some of these: *'So me dad picked me to go on to the cables as they called it. It was part and parcel of the team, and then I stopped on there until I went to shearers, we used to call them, because it was like shearing coal in a round disc and we used to chuck it on an armoured conveyor, panzer as we called it.'*

Many different terms are also given for the identity discs

which miners would carry and pass to the banksmen when entering and leaving the mine to ensure the numbers underground would be known. Gary Brown comments: *'Motties, checks, 'cos you'd got your square tally to go down, your round tally to come up, and your aluminium tally, which was your pay tally. Very important on a Thursday.'* The terms used by our miners were checks, motties, tallies, tags and tokens. Interestingly, these terms were still used in modern mines where swipe cards had been introduced to monitor men entering and leaving the mine.

Life in the mines was very hard, and what got most men through it was the friendship and camaraderie which they felt with those they worked alongside. We mentioned in a previous section that the social aspects of life were also often tied to the mine – sporting events, allotments, brass bands and the like. We also found that men found other outlets for their emotions, and these included making music, painting and writing.

We would like to finish this book with a poem written by Roger Cornish, one of the miners we interviewed as part of the project.

Shelly

You could never forget Shelly,
with his be-bop-a-lu-la
– Gene Vincent at six o'clock on
the manrider train.

The flume of baccy juice at his feet,
an act to the management,
"not too close sunshine",
"don't step on my men."

Brothers underground – carrying Tommy Collier
out the pit twice in a week.
A camaraderie
I grieve to have lost.
I wish I could have spoken to him
in those last days,
joking in his wheelchair,
running the nurses ragged at 63.

I could have told him: thanks for pointing me the right way,
thanks for the humility, the grace and honesty of a real man –
for your hand at my weakest time, for your truth
Shelly – for a friendship hewn in Anthracite.

Now the tools all rodded up,
your snap box empty,
water gone.
Rest now mucca, the ratch is won.

Select Bibliography

BOOKS ON MINING

Bell, David. 2006. *Memories of the Derbyshire Coalfields.*
Newbury: Countryside Books.

Bell, David. 2007. *Memories of the Leicestershire Coalfields.*
Newbury: Countryside Books.

Bell, David. 2008. *Memories of the Nottinghamshire Coalfields.*
Newbury: Countryside Books.

Carswell, Jeanne and Roberts, Tracey. 1992. *Getting the Coal.*
Oxford: The Alden Press.

Cross, Bill. 1995. *Bill of Bulwell.* Warwick: Plowright Press.

Franks, Angela. 2001. *Nottinghamshire Miners' Tales.*
Nottingham: Adlard Print.

Griffin, Alan R. 1971. *Mining in the East Midlands.*
Plymouth: Frank Cass and Company Ltd.

Griffin, Alan R. 1977. *The British Coalmining Industry.*
Retrospect and prospect. Ashbourne: Moorland Publishing.

Tonks, David. 2003. *My Ancestor was a Coal Miner.*
London: Society of Genealogists.

BOOKS ON 'PIT TALK'

Douglass, Dave. 1973. *Pit Talk in County Durham.* Oxford: TruExpress.

Forster, W. 1969. *A Survey of Terms used by Miners in the South Midlands.* Leicester: Vaughan Papers in Adult Education, No. 15.

Gerard, David. 1982. *A glossary of Nottinghamshire dialect and mining terms.* In: Keith Sagar (ed.) A D.H. Lawrence Handbook. Manchester: Manchester University Press, pp. 165–176.

Griffiths, Bill. 2007. *Pitmatic: The talk of the North East Coalfield.* Newcastle: Northumbria University Press.

Hooson, William. 1979. *The Miners Dictionary.* Ilkley: The Scholar Press.

INTERNET RESOURCES

http://www.healeyhero.co.uk:
A collection of resources and memoirs related to mining and mining rescue

http://www.healeyhero.co.uk/rescue/individual/ Bob_Bradley/A-1.html:
Including the history of mining, by Bob Bradley

http://myweb.tiscali.co.uk/coalface/glossary/ aterms.htm:
A glossary of mining terms

https://www.ncm.org.uk/downloads/42/ Mining_Words.pdf:
A mining glossary produced by the National Coal Mining Museum